THE FLUTTERING MOON

Published by

The Fluttering Moon

Edited by Shruti Gupta

Published by : Poetry World Org.

Publisher's Address : Haryana

Printed under PWO in India

Edition : I (2021)

ISBN (Paperback) - 9789390724727

Book Design by POETRY WORLD

THE FLUTTERING MOON

Compiled and Edited By

Shruti Gupta

कवि तड़पता है तभी लिखता है

Hey readers, she is Shruti Gupta daughter of Mr. Rakesh Gupta and Mrs. Anju Gupta. She is from Jammu and is currently pursuing BCom. She has worked in more than 10+ anthologies. Now compiling her very first anthology named "The Fluttering Moon". She tries to express her feelings through her poetries. She believes in living in the present rather than thinking about past or future.

She has been writing for past few months and believes that words too have voice in themselves. Writing is not only her dream but her passion also.

She tries to make her every moment special. "Every difficult step today is for a better tomorrow" is what she believes in. Most of her poetries are based on her true feelings.

You can check her writings on her instagram handle:-

@snwritings_

CHILDHOOD MEMORIES

Bachpan bhi kya zamana tha

Khushiyon ka khazana tha

Chahat chaand ko pane ki thi

Pr dil titli ka deewana tha...

Khabar na thi kch subah ki

Na shaam ka thikana tha

Thak kr aana tha school se

Par khelne bhi jaana tha...

Maa ki kahaniya thi

Pariyon ka fasana tha

Barish me kagaz ki nav thi

Har mousam suhana tha...

Har khel me saathi the

Har rishta nibhana tha

Rone ki wajah na thi

Na tha hasne ka bahana...

Kyu ho gye hum itne bde

Isse acha toh vo bachpan ka zamana tha...

Shruti Gupta

INDEX

BEND BUT DO NOT BREAK

Bend but do not break!
The litmus of eternity,
Will test you each time,
You may turn red or blue,
Or remain neutral.
But you can't abandon yourself,
Midst of inner turmoil
So, absorb and transform. Millions of miles an hour
The smog forge ahead,
Aimless aggressive ardent fury, busting clumps and hurling
things.
But one small spark in vast emptiness
Is enough to make them hope.
 As you sit alone,
Wrap your arms around yourself tight,
And hold throughout out the night,
With blankets of despair at the edge,
Rays of hope would break in filling you with independent
strength.
And at life's crossroads
Stoop down to your roots
 Of which you are a flower of turn to your soil,
 Of which you are part of,
You keep loving them,
 But this time love yourself a little more
 Bend but do not break!

AKANSHA SHARMA

HOPE

Her love was an immense ocean-

He stood there by the shore.

Waiting for the waves to him,

But never to move a step forward.

Every time the waves came in,

He teased and then moved back.

The waves tried hard to touch him,

But were only stuck by his definitive pride.

Soon the mighty sun came down,

Dissolving its light in the ocean-

The ocean so busy chasing a shadow,

Was unaware of what she truly deserved.

By the time she realised her fate

Darkness fell- it was too late.

The man was gone, the sky wept stars,

But the moon came up to lift the waves high.

Anusha Naik

BEST MOMENTS

"I walked into that classroom and my eyes fell on you,
But how our destinies would cross paths, no one knew.
 Walking up to you with no specific intention,
 I was quite surprised at the affection.
Though you tried to convince me you had no feelings,
 It didn't change my love for you.
Though you didn't see it,
It was hurtful to see you love someone else.
 I was persistent, but always withheld
What I felt, I couldn't possibly believe that your flirting
meant nothing.
Though I never expected you to be this loving,
Because finally you confessed,
You had feelings for me though this huge mess,
 I felt hundred different emotions at once,
I didn't know how to respond,
My cheeks were flushed.
I had gained the entire world in one instant,
And nothing could ever make me forget it.
Because I never thought walking into that class, on very
first day,
That boy in the front row with the bright blue eyes,
Would ever make me feel this way".

Baisakhi Das

WHOLE ALONE

There were dark circles around my eyes,

And I was talking to you till 5.

This world never recognized,

But I think your heart was a gem inside.

Life was good going before you,

But when you came, I was falling for you.

You made it all beautiful,

But now as you have gone it has become all ugly.

But as you have gone,

I am whole alone.

This life has taught me so many things,

And now you are in those things to see,

Thank you for giving me a lesson,

Those 5 am were a session.

CHITRA SHETTY

KNOW YOURSELF

Know your worth,

because that's the place from where you'll get your

confidence.

Know your strength,

because that's the place from where you'll get your courage.

Know your friends,

because those are the one's that'll always stay with you.

Know your enemies,

because they are the one's that'll teach you.

But before everything know yourself,

because no one can help you better than you, yourself.

HARSHITA VERMA

MY FIRST TEACHER

Every moment I thank her, every moment I appreciate her,

There is none other, she is my mother.

Fathers are correct but mothers are always right.

She made me believe in love at first sight,

We should never lose hopes in our life,

Once she said always do what's your choice,

During my younger days did my upbringing with

Grace.

I always admired her courage,

Which continuously enhanced my knowledge.

She made me overcome all the fears,

When I entered the teen years,

At every stage she helped me up,

Whenever I have looked down.

A mother is the brilliant master,

She will always nourish you faster.

Literally I really don't need to bother,

Mummy is the best teacher none other!

HAR DEEPANSH BAHADUR SINHA

WHY

Why do we love?
If Life will make us part.
Why do our feelings grow?
If days will change them all.
Why do our heartbeat with warm passion?
If distance between us blows it off.
Why do I give you my heart?
If you don't even, try to start.
Why do you tell me you love me so much?
When you can't care for me enough.
Why do I respond to your touch?
When I can't erase from my heart this fear.
Why can't I stop these painful tears?
Why can't I be cruel to you when you're so near.
Why do you promise?
When you can't make dreams come true.
Why do i still smile to you?
Although the endless pain I go through,
I wonder why?
Why it all had to die.

Kavya Dhar

THE MOON

In the darkness of the sea,

There's a bowl full of courtesy.

Makes the world shine and glow,

Takes the people to another flow.

When the waves touch this bowl,

Gifts it's fireflies and all.

It never loses its own light,

Doesn't matter how much it fights.

It seems full on the sky,

Only the sea shows how it cries.

No one can ever play this way,

Gives it's light, takes darkness away.

If the moon can shine at night,

I can too sparkle in dark times.

I have a sea which knows me well,

But I have to gift it's waves my shells.

Like that bowl gifts it's fireflies,

I'll heal and make others fly.

I'll fight and never lose my light,

Finally, I know how to delight!

MAHAM ANSARI

BLACK

The colour Black,
Black is an ominous colour,
It represents the sign of death and sadness,
It is the colour of the silence, the language in which the
silence utters consequences,
In ebony crowded around a casket void of a whisper.
Black is the colour of the night, full of danger, schemes,
and chaos,
The haunt to cross the sea of endless desire in greed's
fragile canoe,
Just seeing the colour will make you fill with hopelessness
and dread,
Creating a sense of void, something that you cannot escape,
Like a trap, like a cycle,
A cycle of life, that you can never escape.
Black is not only ominous but beautiful,
Like the skin, which can face and overpower through any
amount of discrimination and taunt,
Till it's proved how equality and self-belief can be the
strength of man.
When combined with other colours black is power,
With all colours together brings black, signifying the
strength of unity,
It represents days that were hard and it represents the
colour of struggle to a smile of peace and content.
Black is the colour of life.

Mihika Saraf

MR MOON ON LOVE

"O, hark, beautiful girl!
I am Mr. Moon,
I fly every day to steal your heart soon.
My white dress dazzles in the dark,
I leave hastily by the arrival of lark!
Nightingale is my messenger, who sings my heart to each
stranger.
As the King of gloomy night,
I select my soldiers, stars, to fight.
The girl in my heart stays in the Earth,
She is the goddess of shy and mirth: Her eyes reflect me as
two in it--- Why should I be a fool in sky with hit?
I am Mr. Moon,
I order the river,
Go to her room and turn as rain to shower,
And clouds should be her dress, for our wedding that cures
my long stress.
 Am I a mad to love her with a smile?
It is her who stares me by walking a mile.
I wish to be born as an ugly man in her place,
My love will not fade way in human race.

MR. V. HEYMONTH KUMAR

HAPPINESS

Here and there happiness is,

But no one recognizes where it is.

Every day everyone runs after it,

Almost everyone knows not what it is.

Happiness is found high and low.

But it's not goods to go and purchase from the store.

One great outlook requires for

Seeing, smelling, feeling, and finding it.

Farmers smell it in the paddy field,

Rickshaw men find it in the full passenger's seat,

Pregnant women feel it after giving birth to a baby,

When wage labours always get paid in the evening.

Let's surrender ourselves at our work,

And struggle to achieve it, score it.

Let us steal not others' happiness.

Until we deserve it."

Nayanjyoti Baruah

GIRL CHILD: A BLESSING

Being a girl in a family,

Is a gift from God,

Which he gives you happily,

With a sweet nod,

Too blessed to get,

Which we don't yet,

Her smile gives us happiness,

And her tears fill us with sadness,

Her feet bring a luck,

Which till tucked in something Keep that gift stick to heart,

Ever and ever.

PARAS SHARMA

FLY ABOVE THE CLOUDS

We rise, we fall, we build us up,

We try, we cry but never give up.

The sky's the limit they used to say,

So, we got to reach the sky one day.

Success is a hard-earned term,

My friend to earn it one must run till the end,

From the streets of the old country town.

One must rise targeting the king's crown,

Some might help you along your hard life's way,

While others may pass by blaming your luck is grey.

But you still get up and keep on the fight,

Until you see your success as clear and bright.

Beyond and above the clouds you should rise,

And thank your God as you kiss the prize.

As many of us tried our best but few succeed,

And many gave everything, but few got what they need.

PRITTAM BHATTACHARYYA

THE UNSPOKEN WORDS

I wrote the magical words,

With fear and happiness.

These are the words,

I always want to share with you.

I write it thousand times,

and I shred it hundred times.

I am scared to tell you my feelings,

because you have always told me that,

we are best friends.

I never want to lose our friendship,

I want to hold on it in my heart.

But what can I do? I am falling for you my love.

You are the one with whom I want to share my life.

You always told me; we have not had any secrets.

I write this letter for you and

just like other times, I put it in

my secret box.

I hope you feel my love, and I will wait for you till the end of

my life....

Sujisha Subrahmanian

WHAT IS BEAUTIFUL?

What is truly beautiful?

Not something that you find astonishing for few hours and

forget it.

But something you cherish forever.

MITA DAS

FAKE PEOPLE, SOCIETY

"I don't think wearing a mask and moving outside is difficult to those people who are already habituated to wear a fake mask in public.

We live in a "society" where people say, "Don't judge a book by its cover" but still consider "First impression as the last impression."

MONANGI PRATYUSHA

SELF DIGNITY

Don't assume me like the sun that every day comes to you!

I'm like the marvellous moon.

Who has Mega fan base! Who may make you to wait, until I

decide you to arrive and achieve me!

MR. RAMKUMAR VELUMANI

आने ना देना

यूँ आँखों में अश्क आने ना देना
अपने होठों से मुस्कान जाने ना देना
ज़िन्दगी तो चलती ही रहेगी,
ज़िन्दगी को तुम पर हँसने मत देना

आपकी खैरियत की दुआ रहती है,
कभी हमको ग़लत ना समझना,
हमसफ़र तो नहीं आप हमारे
दिल पर हक़ अपना ही समझना।

ये आपका जन्मदिवस है ,
यूँ ही मुस्कुराते रहना।

Ashish Chauhan

तुम्हे भी है मुझे भी है

साथ तो नहीं ॱ अब
अहसास तुम्हें भी है मुझे भी है
बिखरे हुऐ हम-तुम,
खबर तुम्हें भी है मुझे भी है
हरारत हुई हमें
असर तुम्हें भी है मुझे भी है।
हालत बद से बद्तर हुई
नज़र तुम्हें भी है मुझे भी है,
मिलेंगें फिर हम
ऐसी एक प्यास तुम्हें भी है मुझे भी है।

AMMAR BIN KALEEM

एक कवि हूँ

एक कवि हूँ
ख्यालों का समुंदर लिए,
गमों की गहराइयाँ बहुत
खुशी का बसेरा सिये
कभी ज़ज़्बात कभी एहसास,
बवंडर बन उमड़ते हैं
जाने कितनी बातों को
अल्फ़ाज़ में गिरफ्त किये
एक कवि हूँ।
ख्वाबों का समुंदर लिए
एक कवि हूँ ख्वाबों में डूबी हुई
रात चाँदनी,सुबह शबनमी इन्हीं
बातों में ज़िन्दगी ज़हद को गुंथी हुई
अनगिनत किरदार हैं, अनगिनत हैं कहानियाँ
कुछ हैं हकीक़त तो
कुछ में कल्पना को भाव में
पिरोती हुई
एक कवि हूँ बस
ख्वाबों में डूबी हुई।

Deepshikha Sharma

तुम नहीं हो

यह चाँद है , यह रात है,
पर तुम नहीं हो।
यह लौ है , यह चिराग़ है,
पर तुम नहीं हो।
रात की ख़ामोशियों में ,
बस तुम्हारी
आवाज़ ही आवाज़ है ,
पर तुम नहीं हो।
मेरे कांधे पर तुम्हारे गेसुओं की
छुअन का एहसास है,
पर तुम नहीं हो।
सिरहाने में दबे वो सारे ख़त
आज भी मेरे साथ हैं ,
पर तुम नहीं हो।
सामने की दीवार पर तुम्हारी ,
वो धूमिल- सी तस्वीर ही
मेरी आख़िरी आस है ,
पर तुम नहीं हो।

Deesha Sri

बच्चों से उनका बचपन कभी जुदा ना हो

मेरे लाखों सपने थे
लगते सारे अपने थे, छोटी-छोटी दिक्कत थी
अब समझ न आए वो सपना था या हकीक़त?
स्कूल में बीतता अपना दिन था पूरा
दोस्तों के बिना अपना दिन था अधूरा,
वो छोटी-छोटी बातों पर रूठ जाना
कट्टी-पक्की करके रिश्ता बनाना,
कभी सोचा नहीं था कि ज़िन्दगी ये दिन दिखाएगी
हमारी ज़िन्दगी के सबसे ख़ास पल हमारी याद
बन जाएगी।
बचपन में सोचा करते थे कि बड़े होगे तो ज़िन्दगी
जी पाएँगे
ये तो कभी पता ही नहीं था, कि बड़े होने के बाद
अपने बचपन के लिए तरस जाएगे!
मान लिया आज यह भी कि माँ-बाप से बड़ा न
कोई खुदा हो
मौला अब यही अरदास है तुझसे,
वक्त से पहले न कोई बच्चा अपने बचपन से जुदा
हो
वक्त से पहले न कोई बच्चा अपने बचपन से जुदा
हो।

याद है आज भी कि कैसे रोते-रोते अपनी जींद मनवाते थे

घर वाले हमारी मुस्कान के लिए हर हद से गुज़र जाते थे,

काश वो वक्त कभी खत्म ना होता, तन्हाइयों में छुपकर ये दिल कभी रोया ना होता

माँ-बाप का साया हर बच्चे के सर पर रहे

कोई बच्चा कभी भूखा ना तेरे दर पर रहे।

मान लिया आज यह भी कि माँ-बाप से बड़ा न कोई खुदा हो

मौला अब यही अरदास है तुझसे

वक्त से पहले न कोई बच्चा अपने बचपन से जुदा हो

वक्त से पहले न कोई बच्चा अपने बचपन से जुदा हो।

Goutam Jaitely

इश्क़ का दरिया

मत कहा कर मुझे रुकने को,
मत कहा कर तुझसे बयाँ ना करने को,
इश्क़ का दरिया है यह जनाब,
डुबकी लगाकर, डूबने को कहा करते हैं, तैरने को
नहीं।"

Ritika Sharma

इश्क़ का दरिया

मेरी अधूरी कहानी

"मेरी ज़िन्दगी की अधूरी कहानी सुना था प्यार इंसान की ज़िन्दगी बदल कर रख देता है, और मेरे साथ भी कुछ ऐसा ही हुआ। मेरा प्यार कोई एक दिन, एक हफ़्ते या एक महीने का नहीं था। 11 साल हो गए थे हमें ये रिश्ता निभाते निभाते। जब मिले थे तो पूरा दिन एक दूसरे से बातें करते रहते थे। मैं उसके लिए हर वो चीज़ किया करती थी जो मेरे बस में थी। अपना रिश्ता पूरी ईमानदारी से निभाती थी। शायद वो भी उस समय ये रिश्ता ईमानदारी से निभाता था, नहीं तो ये रिश्ता इतने वर्ष कैसे निभता। बहुत सी मुश्किलें आयी जीवन में पर मैंने उसका हाथ कभी नहीं छोड़ा। ज़माने से लड़ी पर उसका हाथ थाम रखा। उसने भी मेरा हर क़दम पर साथ दिया। आदत सी हो गई थी उसकी अगर एक घंटा भी बात न होती तो मन बेचैन सा हो जाता था। बिना गलती के उसे मनाना पड़े तो मैं मनाती थी, उसकी हर छोटी-छोटी चीज़ों का ख़्याल रखने लग गई थी। पता ही नहीं चला रिश्ता कब

इतना गहरा होता गया कि कब वो मेरी ज़िन्दगी बन गया। पर कहते है ना कि ज़रूरत से ज़्यादा कर चीज़ विनाशकारी होती है। इतने खूबसूरत रिश्ते को न जाने किसकी नज़र लग गई। ९ साल बाद ज़िन्दगी में ऐसा दिन आया कि उसने हमारे रिश्ते को भूला दिया। वो किसी और लड़की को अपनी ज़िन्दगी में ले आया और मैं इस बात से बिल्कुल अंजान थी। जब सच पता चला तो पैरों तले ज़मीन खिसक गई थी। ऐसा लगता था कि मैंने सब कुछ खो दिया। अकेले रहना शुरू ही किया था कि वो लौट आया। उसने अपनी गलती के लिए माफ़ी माँगी। शायद मैं ही पागल थी जो उसे माफ़ कर दिया। पर कभी अब वो बात नहीं लगती। कहते है ना कि जो लोग एक बार दगा करते है वो दोबारा भी कर सकते है। उसने फिर वही किया दोबारा अपनी ज़िन्दगी में किसी और को ले आया। मैं समझ चुकी थी कि अब ये वो इंसान नहीं जिससे मैंने प्यार किया था। बस उस दिन ऐसा लगा जैसे अब कुछ नहीं बचा। बस तब से मन के हर ख़्याल को कागज़ पर कलम से लिखना शुरू कर दिया।

आज इतने महीने हो गए लेकिन उसकी याद वैसी कि वैसी ही है। क्यों वफ़ा करके भी मेरी ज़िन्दगी की कहानी अंधेरी रह गई। क्या शिकायत करें अब उससे जब वो मेरी किस्मत में था ही नहीं। और इसी के साथ मेरे जीवन कि कहानी अधूरी रह गई।

Rashmi Baweja

मेरे अल्फ़ाज़

कसूर सिर्फ नज़र का था
शरारात दिल में हुई थी
खुशनुमा हर पल हुआ था
इबादत सजदें मे हुई थी,
हर दुआ मैं थी वो शामिल
मुलाकात फिर उससे हुई थी।
इशारों मे दोस्ती हुई
और बातें नज़रों में हुई थी
वहीं मेरी ज़िंदगी बनी और
ख्वाबों में भी इल्तिजा हुई
और फ़िर एक दिन
तन्हाई ने दस्तक दी ......
चारों और खामोशी छाई रही
सब खत्म सा हो गया
ना जाने कहाँ खोया रहा मैं
हर कोई मुझसे ख़फ़ा हो गया
सोचा खत्म कर लूं खुद को
पर फिर से इश्क़ किया मैंने
और खुद से इश्क़ करना ज़िंदगी और मौत ढोनों से
बेहतर रहा।"

RONIT KUMAWA

Morden Bahu

सर पर पल्ला ना सही ,
आँखों में हया और लाज तो है,

कंगन, बिछिया ना सही ,
परिवार की परंपरा का ख्याल तो है ....

झाड़ू, पोछा ना भी करती हो ,
बड़ों की परवाह और प्यार तो है,

साड़ी में लिपटी ना सही ,
बड़ों की इज्ज़त और सम्मान तो है ....

घूमना फिरना life style में शामिल सही,
पर त्यौहारों की जान तो है ,

मंदिर में हर रोज़ ना जाती हो
पर भक्ति भाव मन में तो है।

Ritu Singodia

तेरा खत

चंद कागज़ के टुकड़ों पे महके वो अपनी खुशबू
भेज दो
खत में उकेर के लफ्जों की अपनी तस्वीर हूबहू भेज
दो।

Sushil Pradhan

वो चाँद से ज़्यादा हसीन (ग़ज़ल)

चाँद की चाँदनी से भी ज़्यादा हसीन है,
कहकशाँ से भी प्यारी इक मेहजबीन है,

चाँद भी हैरान हो जायेगा तुम्हे देखकर,
मुझे अक्स तुम्हारा लगता जैसे शाहीन है,

चाँद के नूर की तारीफ़ सब करते है मगर,
मुझे चाँद से ज़्यादा तुम्हारा नूर आफ़रीन है,

अगर तू चाँद है मेरा तो मै चाँद का दाग़ हूँ,
गर मै नाज़ करूँ खुद पर तो तू नाज़नीन है,

कुछ इस कदर इश्क़ करता है जुनैद तुमसे,
कि इस दुनिया मे मौजूद जितनी ज़मीन है।

Sheikh Mohommad Junaid

चाँदनी रात में (ग़ज़ल)

अब तलक अधूरी हैं उसने छेड़ी थी जो बात चाँदनी रात में

आज शिद्दत से याद आई पहली मुलाकात चाँदनी रात में

रात की स्याही ने लिखे कई ज़ज़्बात दोनों ही दिलों पर ....

धीमे धीमे हुई थी एक मोहब्बत की शुरुआत चाँदनी रात में

खूबसूरत सी एक फ़िज़ा में चाँद की मद्धम रोशनी के तले   उसने

पेश की मुझे नर्म जज़्बों की सौगात चाँदनी रात में

शब -ए- इश्क़ में भिगोया था उसने जिन फुहारों से मुझे....

कभी बरसे मुझ पर वही प्यार की बरसात चाँदनी रात में

कुछ हँसी पल गुज़रे हुए जो कभी वो फिर मेरे नाम करे

मैं रखु उससे दिल समेटने की दरख्वास्त चाँदनी रात में

Shadab Jahan

43